# Crock Pot Cookbook for Beginners

*The ultimate guide with 50 recipes for beginners. Cook like a pro and wow your friends with amazing low fat dishes. Lose up to 7 pounds in 7 days*

*Clara Smith*

# Table of Contents

# Introduction

The crockpot has long been a favorite kitchen implement for the 'set-it-and-forget-it' meal. It's a wonderful invention by whoever thought it up, and it has saved many a few dollars on electricity by not needing to keep the stove and oven on for extended hours and all day. So, what really is a crockpot?

The crockpot slow cooking method involves basically depositing the ingredients you desire to cook into the crockpot bowl (usually by stirring it with a wooden spoon or a ladle), adding the liquid of choice, cooking it for a few hours until it's done. These used to be the standard cooking methods in kitchens, and they have stayed the same with the invention of the crockpot. Nowadays, most crockpots have interiors thermostatically controlled to ensure that it's set at the right temperature during the cooking process to not over-cook your meals.

The best in crockpot slow cooking is finding that low and slow recipe. Recipes that are low in time length are usually very low in steps, and not much work is involved. It usually leads to the much sought after 'set it and forget it' kind of meal. Imagine not having to watch your meals cook slowly as you work on other tasks; you can avoid the temptation of peeking or checking on it too often and not having to worry about burning or crusting on the sides of your crockpot. When cooking at low heat, you don't have to worry about your meal exploding all over the kitchen or all the grease falling out and sticking to the bottom of your crock.

The best use of crockpot slow cooking is the convenience of the food, especially during holidays and parties. You can set the crockpot down on the table, and everyone can serve themselves. It is an excellent and great way to spend time with your guests and treat them well. There is nothing cheesier than eating the same dish fondue style. You get to enjoy slow cooking hotdogs for hours and hours without little ones surreptitiously taking off the top and poaching them in the pool of oil sitting beside the dish.

A crockpot is a very good way to use leftovers for a delicious meal. If you cook a large meal regularly and you have leftovers, put them in a crockpot with a liquid and let it cook. It will double the amount of food leftover or fed to the cat at the end of the week.

Crockpot cooking generally saves time, but it is also a low-budget way to cook. Slow cooking food can save you money because they are usually very low and easy to make. In fact, it is even possible to cook a meal with the last few pennies in your wallet. If you're on a tight budget and you don't have much to spend on your meals, the crockpot is the way to go.

Crockpots even make for a great gift since it's made in many shapes and sizes, from the really small, 1-quart crockpot to the huge 8 quarts or more. Any shape or size would be a welcome gift for anyone because everyone eats. Any occasion could be a good time to give someone a crockpot, and the more occasions you can name, the more crockpots you could make as gifts.

Crockpots are a good thing for singles who do not have many friends, and getting together can be difficult. You can go on cooking and not having to worry about cooking for anyone. You also don't have to go through the motions of doing a dinner party or charity work every week. You could just throw some ingredients together in your crockpot, turn it on and leave. That way, you're free to do whatever you like while your crockpot cooks your meal.

To whom is this cookbook? This cookbook is for people who want to spend less time in the kitchen and less money on food. This cookbook is also for people who wish to cook their meals in a healthy manner or for people with little time or money, and lastly, this is for people who enjoy sharing meals with friends and family. Treat your guests to a good meal every day. Slow cooking, live long!

## CHAPTER 1:

# Breakfast

## 1.   Cheesy Bacon Hash Browns

Preparation time: 5 minutes

Cooking time: 3 hours

Servings: 7

Ingredients:

- 1-pound hash browns, thawed

- 1 can cream of mushroom soup

- ¼ cup milk

- ½ pound sharp cheddar cheese, grated

- 10 slices of bacon, cook until crispy

Directions:

1. Place the hash browns in the crockpot. Add the cream of mushroom soup and milk. Add the cheese on top. Close the lid and cook on low for 4 hours. Sprinkle with cheese on top.

Nutrition:

Calories: 362

Carbohydrates: 14.6g

Protein: 14.5g

Fat: 27.4g

Fiber:1.5 g

# 2.     Hodgepodge Omelet

Preparation time: 5 minutes

Cooking time: 5 hours

Servings: 2

Ingredients:

- 2 eggs, beaten

- ¼ cup milk

- 2 cooked turkey sausages, chopped

- 1 cup button mushrooms, chopped

- 1 red bell pepper, julienned

Directions:

1. In a mixing bowl, combine the eggs and milk. Season with salt and pepper to taste. Place the egg mixture and stir in the sausages, mushrooms, and bell pepper.

2. Close the lid and cook on low for 5 hours. Sprinkle

   with chopped green onions on top.

Nutrition:

Calories: 332

Carbohydrates: 17.85g

Protein: 27.7g

Fat: 17.07g

## 3. Basic Overnight Quinoa and Oats

Preparation time: 5 minutes Cooking time: 5 hours

Servings: 8

Ingredients:

- 1 ½ cups steel-cut oats

- ½ cup quinoa 4 ½ cups evaporated milk

- 4 tablespoons maple syrup

- 1 teaspoon vanilla extract

Directions:

1. Stir in all ingredients in the crockpot. Close the lid and cook on low for 7 hours. Top with your favorite topping.

Nutrition:Calories:194 Carbohydrates: 31.8g Protein:8.9 g Fat: 6.9g

# 4.  **Breakfast Quiche**

Preparation Time: 10 minutes

Cooking Time: 3 hours 30 minutes

Servings: 6

Ingredients:

- 5 eggs, lightly beaten

- 1/8 tsp nutmeg

- 1 cup green onions, sliced

- 1 cup cheddar cheese, grated

- 2 cups broccoli florets

- Pepper

- Salt

Directions:

1. Spray the inside of a crock pot with cooking spray. In a mixing bowl, beat eggs with pepper, nutmeg, and salt. Add cheese and broccoli to the egg mixture and stir well.

2. Pour egg mixture into the crock pot. Cover and cook on high for 3 hours. Add green onions to the top of the quiche, cover and cook on low for 30 minutes longer. Serve and enjoy.

Nutrition:

Calories 144

Fat 10 g

Carbohydrates 3.8 g

Protein 10.5 g

# 5.    Egg Sausage Breakfast Casserole

Preparation Time: 10 minutes

Cooking Time: 4 hours

Servings: 8

Ingredients:

- 10 eggs

- 3 garlic cloves, minced

- 3/4 cup whipping cream

- 1 cup cheddar cheese, shredded

- 12 oz sausage, cooked and sliced

- 2 cups broccoli, chopped

- 1/4 tsp pepper

- 1/2 tsp salt

Directions:

1. Spray the inside of a crock pot with cooking spray. Layer half the sausage, half the broccoli, and half the shredded cheese in a crock pot. Repeat with remaining sausage, broccoli, and cheese.

2. In a mixing bowl, whisk eggs, garlic, whipping cream, pepper, and salt until combined. Pour egg mixture over layered mixture. Cover and cook on low for 4 hours or until center is set. Serve and enjoy.

Nutrition:

Calories 322

Fat 25.8 g

Carbohydrates 2.9 g

Protein 19.7 g

# CHAPTER 2:

# Mains

## 6.    Banana Chicken Curry

Preparation time: 15 minutes

Cooking time: 7 hours

Servings: 6

Ingredients:

- 2 pounds chicken drumsticks

- 1 jalapeno pepper, chopped

- 1 banana, sliced  1 1/2 cups diced tomatoes

- 1 large onion, chopped  4 garlic cloves, chopped

- 1 teaspoon cumin powder

- 1 teaspoon curry powder

- 1/4 cup dry white wine

- 1 bay leaf 1 lemongrass stalk, crushed

- 1 cup coconut milk

- Salt and pepper to taste

Directions:

1. Combine the chicken, jalapeno, banana, tomatoes, onion, garlic, spices, wine, bay leaf, lemongrass and coconut milk in a Crock Pot.

2. Add salt and pepper to taste and cook on low settings for 7 hours. Serve the curry warm or chilled.

Nutrition: Calories: 451 Carbs: 56g Fat: 7g Protein: 42g

# 7.    White Bean Cassoulet

Preparation time: 15 minutes

Cooking time: 6 hours

Servings: 6

Ingredients:

- 2 tablespoons olive oil

- 1 large onion, chopped

- 2 carrots, diced

- 1 parsnip, diced

- 2 garlic cloves, chopped

- 2 cans white beans, drained

- 1 cup vegetable stock

- 1 thyme sprig

- 1 1/2 cups diced tomatoes

- 1 bay leaf

- Salt and pepper to taste

Directions:

1. Heat the oil in a skillet and add the onion, carrot and garlic. Sauté for 2 minutes until softened and translucent then transfer in your Crock Pot.

2. Add the remaining ingredients and cook on low settings for 6 hours. Serve the cassoulet warm.

Nutrition:

Calories: 79

Carbs: 15g

Fat: 1g

Protein: 4g

# 8.   Spiced Pork Belly

Preparation time: 15 minutes

Cooking time: 7 hours

Servings: 6

Ingredients:

- 3 pounds piece of pork belly

- 1 tablespoon cumin powder

- 1 tablespoon brown sugar

- 1 teaspoon chili powder

- 1 teaspoon grated ginger

- 1 tablespoon molasses

- 2 garlic cloves, minced

- 1 tablespoon soy sauce

- 1/2 cup white wine

Directions:

1. Mix the cumin powder, sugar, chili powder, ginger, molasses, garlic and soy sauce in a bowl. Spread this mixture over the pork belly and rub it well into the skin and meat.

2. Place the belly in your crock pot and add the wine. Cook on low settings for 7 hours. Serve the belly warm with your favorite side dish.

Nutrition:

Calories: 518

Carbs: 0g

Fat: 53g

Protein: 9g

# 9.    Jamaican Jerk Chicken

Preparation time: 15 minutes

Cooking time: 7 hours

Servings: 4

Ingredients:

- 4 chicken breasts

- 2 tablespoons jerk seasoning

- 2 tablespoons olive oil

- 1/2 cup chicken stock

- 1/4 cup brewed coffee

- 1 jalapeno pepper, chopped

- Salt and pepper to taste

Directions:

1. Season the chicken with salt, pepper and jerk seasoning. Combine the seasoned chicken, stock and coffee, as well as jalapeno pepper in your Crock Pot.

2. Cover with a lid and cook on low settings for 7 hours. Serve the chicken warm and fresh.

Nutrition:

Calories: 324

Carbs: 11g

Fat: 21g

Protein: 21g

## 10.  Saucy Ranch Pork Chops

Preparation Time: 5 minutes Cooking Time: 9 hours

Servings: 6

Ingredients:

- 6 pork loin chops 2 cans condensed cream of chicken soup

- 1 cup milk 1 envelope ranch salad dressing

- Salt and pepper to taste

Directions:

1. Sear the pork loin chops on a hot skillet for at least 3 minutes on all sides. Place all ingredients in the crockpot. Give a good stir. Close the lid and cook on low for 9 hours.

Nutrition: Calories: 451 Carbohydrates:10.5 g Protein: 44.4g Fat: 24.8g

# 11.    Barbecue Pulled Pork

Preparation Time: 5 minutes Cooking Time: 12 hours

Servings: 4

Ingredients:

- 1 ½ pounds pork loin fillet

- 1 can Dr. Pepper's cola

- 1 bottle barbecue sauce

- 1 bay leaf Salt and pepper to taste

Directions:

1. Place all ingredients in the crockpot. Give a good stir. Close the lid and cook on low for 12 hours. Use two forks to shred the meat. Serve on a sandwich.

Nutrition:Calories: 348 Carbohydrates: 43g Protein: 25g Fat: 8g

## 12. Cranberry Pork Chops and Sweet Potatoes

Preparation Time: 10 minutes

Cooking Time: 12 hours

Servings: 6

Ingredients:

- 6 pork chops

- 1 2/3 cups applesauce

- 3 pounds sweet potatoes

- 1 can cranberry sauce

- ¼ cup packed brown sugar

Directions:

1. Season the pork chops with salt and pepper to taste. Place in a skillet heated over high flame and sear on all

sides. Place in the crockpot and pour the rest of the ingredients.

2. Add water if the consistency is too thick. Close the lid and cook on low for 12 hours.

Nutrition:

Calories: 649

Carbohydrates: 101g

Protein: 31g

Fat: 14g

# CHAPTER 3:

# Sides

## 13.    Beans and Red Peppers

Preparation time: 15 minutes

Cooking Time: 2 hours

Servings: 2

Ingredients:

- 2 cups green beans, halved

- 1 red bell pepper, cut into strips

- Salt and black pepper to the taste

- 1 tbsp olive oil

- 1 and ½ tbsp honey mustard

Directions:

1. Add green beans, honey mustard, red bell pepper, oil, salt, and black to Crock Pot. Put the crock pot's lid on and set the cooking time to 2 hours on High settings. Serve warm.

Nutrition:

Calories: 50

Fat: 0g

Carbs: 8g

Protein: 2g

# 14.   Squash Side Salad

Preparation time: 15 minutes

Cooking Time: 4 Hours

Servings: 8

Ingredients:

- 1 tablespoon olive oil

- 1 cup carrots, chopped

- 1 yellow onion, chopped

- 1 teaspoon sugar

- 1 and ½ teaspoons curry powder

- 1 garlic clove, minced

- 1 big butternut squash, peeled and cubed

- A pinch of sea salt and black pepper

- ¼ teaspoon ginger, grated

- ½ teaspoon cinnamon powder

- 3 cups coconut milk

Directions:

1. In your Crock Pot, mix oil with carrots, onion, sugar, curry powder, garlic, squash, salt, pepper, ginger, cinnamon and coconut milk, stir well, cover and cook on Low for 4 hours. Stir, divide between plates and serve as a side dish.

Nutrition:

Calories 200

Fat 4g

Carbs 17g

Protein 4g

# 15.  Creamy Coconut Potatoes

Preparation time: 15 minutes

Cooking Time: 4 Hours

Servings: 2

Ingredients:

- ½ pound gold potatoes, halved and sliced

- 2 scallions, chopped

- 1 tablespoon avocado oil

- 2 ounces coconut milk

- ¼ cup veggie stock

- Salt and black pepper to the taste

- 1 tablespoons parsley, chopped

Directions:

1.  In your Crock Pot, mix the potatoes with the scallions and the other ingredients, toss, put the lid on and cook on High for 4 hours. Divide the mix between plates and serve.

Nutrition:

Calories 306

Fat 14g

Carbs 15g

Protein 12g

# 16. Cauliflower Rice and Spinach

Preparation time: 15 minutes

Cooking Time: 3 Hours

Servings: 8

Ingredients:

- 2 garlic cloves, minced

- 2 tablespoons butter, melted

- 1 yellow onion, chopped

- ¼ teaspoon thyme, dried

- 3 cups veggie stock

- 20 ounces spinach, chopped

- 6 ounces coconut cream

- Salt and black pepper to the taste

- 2 cups cauliflower rice

Directions:

1. Heat up a pan with the butter over medium heat, add onion, stir and cook for 4 minutes. Add garlic, thyme and stock, stir, cook for 1 minute more and transfer to your Crock Pot.

2. Add spinach, coconut cream, cauliflower rice, salt and pepper, stir a bit, cover and cook on High for hours. Divide between plates and serve as a side dish.

Nutrition:

Calories 200

Fat 4g

Carbs 8g

Protein 2g

# 17. Brussels Sprouts And Cauliflower

Preparation time: 15 minutes

Cooking Time: 4 Hours

Servings: 2

Ingredients:

- 1 cup Brussels sprouts, trimmed and halved

- 1 cup cauliflower florets

- 1 tablespoon olive oil

- 1 cup veggie stock

- 2 tablespoons tomato paste

- 1 teaspoon chili powder

- ½ teaspoon ginger powder

- A pinch of salt and black pepper

- 1 tablespoon thyme, chopped

Directions:

1. In your Crock Pot, mix the Brussels sprouts with the cauliflower, oil, stock and the other ingredients, toss, put the lid on and cook on Low for 4 hours. Divide the mix between plates and serve as a side dish.

Nutrition:

Calories 100

Fat 4g

Carbs 8g

Protein 3g

# CHAPTER 4:

# Seafood

## 18.  Cod Platter

Preparation Time: 10 minutes

Cooking Time: 4 hours

Servings: 6

Ingredients:

- 1 ½ lb. cherry tomatoes halved

- 2 ½ tablespoons of fresh rosemary, diced

- 6 (4-oz.) cod fillets

- 3 garlic cloves, minced

- 2 tablespoon of olive oil

- Salt and black pepper, to taste

Directions:

1. Start by throwing all the fixings into your Crockpot. Cover its lid and cook for 4 hours on Low setting. Once done, remove its lid and give it a stir. Serve warm.

Nutrition:

Calories 335

Fat 5.4 g

Carbs 2.1 g

Protein 18.5 g

# 19.    Dinner Mussels

Preparation Time: 10 minutes

Cooking Time: 3 hours

Servings: 8

Ingredients:

- 2 tablespoons of olive oil

- 2 medium yellow onions, diced

- 1 teaspoon of rosemary, dried, crushed

- 2 garlic cloves, minced

- 2 cups of chicken broth

- 4 lbs. mussels, cleaned and de-bearded

- ¼ cup of fresh lemon juice

- Salt and black pepper, to taste

Directions:

1. Start by throwing all the fixings into your Crockpot. Cover its lid and cook for 3 hours on Low setting. Once done, remove its lid and give it a stir. Serve warm.

Nutrition:

Calories 238

Fat 9.5 g

Carbs 1.8 g

Protein 34.2 g

# 20. Butter-Dipped Lobsters

Preparation Time: 10 minutes

Cooking Time: 1 hour

Servings: 8

Ingredients:

- 1 cup of water

- 4 lbs. lobster tails, cut in half

- 4 tablespoons of unsalted butter, melted

- Salt to taste  Black pepper to taste

Directions:

1. Start by throwing all the fixings into your Crockpot. Cover its lid and cook for 1 hour on Low setting. Once done, remove its lid and give it a stir. Serve warm.

Nutrition: Calories 324 Fat 20.7 g Carbs 8.6 g  Protein 15.3 g

# 21. Creamy Lobster

Preparation Time: 10 minutes

Cooking Time: 1 hour

Servings: 8

Ingredients:

- 1½ cups of water

- 4 lbs. fresh lobster tails

- 2 teaspoons of old bay seasoning

- 1 cup of mayonnaise

- 2 scallions, diced

- ¼ cup of unsalted butter, melted

- 4 tablespoons of fresh lemon juice

Directions:

1. Start by throwing all the fixings into your Crockpot except mayonnaise. Cover its lid and cook for 1 hour on Low setting.

2. Once done, remove its lid and give it a stir. Peel the slow-cooked lobster tail and transfer the meat to a bowl. Mix the meat with mayonnaise in that bowl. Garnish as desired. Serve warm.

Nutrition:

Calories 349

Fat 31.9 g

Carbs 6.6 g

Protein 11 g

## 22. Citrus Enriched Salmon

Preparation Time: 10 minutes

Cooking Time: 2 hours

Servings: 6

Ingredients:

- 6 (4-oz.) salmon fillets

- 1 ½ teaspoon of fresh ginger, minced

- 1 ½ tablespoon of olive oil

- 1 ½ cup of white wine

- 4 tablespoons of fresh lemon juice

- 2 ½ teaspoons of fresh orange zest, grated finely

- Black pepper, to taste

- Fresh herbs (garnish)

Directions:

1. Start by throwing all the fixings into your Crockpot. Cover its lid and cook for 2 hours on Low setting. Once done, remove its lid and give it a stir. Garnish with cilantro. Serve warm.

Nutrition:

Calories 487

Fat 37.4 g

Carbs 10.6 g

Protein 28.1 g

## CHAPTER 5:

# Poultry

## 23.   Chicken Stew Marsala

Preparation time: 15 minutes Cooking time: 6-8 hours & 10

minutesServings: 2

Ingredients:

- 1 cup chicken broth

- 1 pound lean chicken leg, cubed

- 2 cups sliced mushrooms

- ¼ – ½ cup Marsala wine or chicken broth

- ¼ – ½ teaspoon crushed dried rosemary leaves

- ¼ cup cold water

- 2 cloves garlic, minced

- 2 tablespoons cornstarch

- Salt and pepper, to taste

Directions:

1. Combine all ingredients, except cornstarch, water, salt, and pepper, in your Crockpot. Cover and cook on low 6 to 8 hours.

2. Cook on high for 10 minutes. Add in the cornstarch and water and stir for 2 to 3 minutes. Season to taste with salt and pepper.

Nutrition:Calories: 347 Carbs: 14g Fat: 22g  Protein: 23g

# 24.  Chicken Biriyani

Preparation time: 15 minutes

Cooking time: 6-8 hours

Servings: 4

Ingredients:

- 1 pound boneless lean chicken leg

- 1 cup chicken broth

- 3 cups cooked basmati or jasmine rice, warm

- 1 clove garlic, minced

- 2 cups chopped onions

- 1 teaspoon ground coriander

- ¾ cup reduced-fat plain yogurt

- ½ teaspoon chili powder

- ¼ teaspoon each: ground cinnamon, cloves

- 1 teaspoon ginger

- 1 tablespoon cornstarch

- Salt and pepper, to taste

Directions:

1. Combine all ingredients, except yogurt, cornstarch, salt, pepper, and rice, in crock pot. Cover and cook on low 6 to 8 hours.

2. Stir in cornstarch and yogurt, and rice. Keep tossing and stirring for 2 to 3 minutes. Season to taste with salt and pepper.

Nutrition:

Calories: 200

Carbs: 57g Fat: 12g Protein: 19g

# 25.   Three-Meat Goulash

Preparation time: 15 minutes

Cooking time: 6-8 hours

Servings: 8

Ingredients:

- 12 ounces cubed (1 inch) boneless chicken breast

- 12 ounces cubed (1 inch) boneless beef eye of round steak

- 12 ounces cubed (1 inch) boneless pork loin

- 1 cup fat-free beef broth

- 3 large tomatoes, coarsely chopped

- ¼ cup tomato paste

- ½ cup each: thinly sliced green onions, chopped onion

- 8 ounces sliced mushrooms

- 1 tablespoon paprika

- ½ teaspoon dried dill weed

- ¾ teaspoon crushed caraway seeds

- ¾ cup reduced-fat sour cream

- 3 tablespoons cornstarch

- 1 pound noodles, cooked, warm

- Salt and pepper, to taste

Directions:

1. Combine all ingredients except sour cream, cornstarch, salt, pepper, and noodles, in 6-quart Crockpot. Cover, cook on low 6 to 8 hours.

2. Combine the sour cream and cornstarch and stir until thickened, approximately for 2 to 3 minutes. Season to taste with salt and pepper. Serve over noodles.

Nutrition: Calories: 326  Carbs: 13g  Fat: 21g  Protein: 20g

# 26.   Chicken Meatball Soup

Preparation time: 15 minutes

Cooking time: 3-4 hours

Servings: 8

Ingredients:

- 2 quarts chicken broth 1 cup chopped onion

- 1 cup thickly sliced carrots, 1 cup zucchini

- Salt and pepper, to taste

- Chicken Meatballs

Directions:

1. Toss in all the ingredients except salt and pepper, in 6-quart crock pot. Cover and cook on high 3 to 4 hours. Season to taste with salt and pepper.

Nutrition: Calories: 250  Carbs: 30g  at: 7g  Protein: 19g

# 27.  Crockpot Chicken Curry

Preparation time: 3 minutes Cooking time: 8 hours

Servings:  6

Ingredients:

- 2 pounds chicken breasts, bones removed

- 1 can coconut milk

- 1 onion, chopped

- 4 tablespoons curry powder Salt and pepper to taste

Directions:

1. Place all ingredients in the crockpot. Give a good stir
   to incorporate everything. Close the lid and cook on
   low for 8 hours or 6 hours on high.

Nutrition: Calories:468 Carbohydrates: 9g Protein: 34.5g Fat:
33.7g

# CHAPTER 6:

# Meat

## 28.   Pork and Okra

Preparation time: 10 minutes

Cooking time: 6 hours

Servings: 2

Ingredients:

- 1 pound pork stew meat, cubed

- 1 cup okra, sliced

- 2 teaspoons olive oil

- 1 red onion, chopped

- ¼ cup beef stock

- ½ teaspoon chili powder

- ½ teaspoon turmeric powder

- 1 cup tomato passata

- A pinch of salt and black pepper

Directions:

1. In your crock pot, combine the pork with the okra, oil and the other ingredients, toss, put the lid on and cook on High for 6 hours. Divide the mix between plates and serve.

Nutrition: Calories 264 Fat 14g Carbs 7g Protein 15g

## 29.   Easy Chives Lamb

Preparation time: 10 minutes

Cooking time: 4 hours

Servings: 2

Ingredients:

- 1 pound lamb chops

- ½ cup chives, chopped

- ½ cup tomato passata

- 2 scallions, chopped

- 2 teaspoons olive oil

- 2 garlic cloves, minced

- ½ teaspoon sweet paprika

- 1 teaspoon cumin, ground

- A pinch of salt and black pepper

Directions:

1. In your crock pot, mix the lamb chops with the chives, passata and the other ingredients, toss, put the lid on and cook on High for 4 hours, Divide the mix between plates and serve.

Nutrition:

Calories 263

Fat 12g

Carbs 6g

Protein 16g

# 30.  Oregano Beef

Preparation time: 10 minutes

Cooking time: 4 hours

Servings: 2

Ingredients:

- 1 pound beef stew meat, cubed

- 1 tablespoon olive oil

- 1 tablespoon balsamic vinegar

- ½ tablespoon lemon juice

- 1 tablespoon oregano, chopped

- ½ cup tomato sauce

- 1 red onion, chopped

- A pinch of salt and black pepper

- ½ teaspoon chili powder

Directions:

1. In your crock pot, mix the beef with the oil, vinegar, lemon juice and the other ingredients, toss, put the lid on and cook on High for 4 hours. Divide the mix between plates and serve right away.

Nutrition:

Calories 263

Fat 14g

Carbs 6g

Protein 18g

# 31.   Pork with Green Beans

Preparation time: 10 minutes

Cooking time: 6 hours

Servings: 2

Ingredients:

- 1 pound pork stew meat, cubed

- 1 tablespoon balsamic vinegar

- 1 cup green beans, trimmed and halved

- 1 tablespoon lime juice

- 1 tablespoon avocado oil

- ½ teaspoon rosemary, dried

- A pinch of salt and black pepper

- 1 cup beef stock

- 1 tablespoon chives, chopped

Directions:

1. In your crock pot, mix the pork stew meat with the green beans, vinegar and the other ingredients, toss, put the lid on and cook on Low for 6 hours. Divide the mix between plates and serve.

Nutrition:

Calories 264

Fat 14g

Carbs 6g

Protein 17g

## 32.   BBQ Ribs

Preparation time: 15 minutes

Cooking Time: 4 Hours

Servings: 4

Ingredients:

- 1-pound pork ribs, roughly chopped

- 1 teaspoon minced garlic

- ½ cup BBQ sauce

- 1 tablespoon olive oil

- ¼ cup plain yogurt

Directions:

1. Mix BBQ sauce with plain yogurt and minced garlic and pour it in the Crock Pot. Then pour olive oil in the skillet and heat well.

2. Add pork ribs and roast them for minutes per side on high heat. Transfer the pork ribs in the Crock Pot and carefully mix. Close the lid and cook them on High for 4 hours.

Nutrition:

Calories 398

Protein 31g

Carbohydrates 12.6g

Fat 23.9g

# CHAPTER 7:

# Vegetables

## 33.    Saag Aloo

Preparation time: 15 minutes

Cooking time: 2 hours & 30 minutes

Servings: 4

Ingredients:

- 24 oz potatoes

- 10 oz spinach

- 1 onion

- 1 teaspoon cumin

- 1 teaspoon ground coriander

Directions:

1. Peel and chop up the potatoes, and add them into the crock pot with 1 ½ oz of water. Peel and slice up the onion, and add it in too.

2. Sprinkle in the cumin and coriander, and season well with salt and pepper. Top with the spinach and cook on High for 2 hours and 30 minutes.

Nutrition:

Calories: 405

Carbs: 33g

Fat: 25g

Protein: 6g

# 34.   Cheese & Tomato Pasta

Preparation time: 15 minutes

Cooking time: 2 hours & 20 minutes

Servings: 4

Ingredients:

- 56 oz canned tomatoes

- 16 oz penne pasta

- 2 teaspoons dried basil

- 1-3/4 cups mozzarella

- 1 onion

Directions:

1. Mix the dried basil and a good pinch of salt and pepper into the canned tomatoes and pour them into the crock

pot. Peel and dice the onion and stir it in too. Cook on Low for 2 hours.

2. Meanwhile, cook the penne according the package directions, and then stir it through the tomato sauce. Shred the mozzarella on top of the dish and cook for a further 20 minutes.

Nutrition:

Calories: 518

Carbs: 68g

Fat: 19g

Protein: 18g

## 35.  Sweet Potato & Coconut Curry

Preparation time: 15 minutes

Cooking time: 7 hours & 5 minutes

Servings: 6

Ingredients:

- 35 oz sweet potatoes

- 14 oz coconut milk

- 3 garlic cloves

- 2 red chilies

- 2 tablespoons peanut butter

Directions:

1. Mince the garlic into a pan and begin softening it for just a minute or 2. De-seed and slice up the chilies, and add them into the pan too, until they become fragrant.

2.  Peel and dice up the sweet potatoes, and add them into the pan just for 5 minutes to begin browning. Stir them around well.

3.  Add the potato mixture into the crock pot, and pour the coconut milk in too. Top up with 8-10 oz of water, seasoned well with salt and pepper. Cook on High for 7 hours.

Nutrition:

Calories: 291

Carbs: 25g

Fat: 14g

Protein: 19g

# 36. Butternut Squash & Cider Stew

Preparation time: 15 minutes

Cooking time: 5 hours

Servings: 6

Ingredients:

- 24 oz peeled butternut squash

- 2 garlic cloves

- 1-1/2 cups apple cider

- 1 cup canned tomatoes

- 1 teaspoon garam masala

Directions:

1. Dice up the squash and add it into a pan with a little water, salt and pepper to begin browning. Mince in the

garlic and sprinkle on the garam masala and stir everything around together.

2. Add everything into the crock pot, and pour in the cider and tomatoes. Cover and cook on Low for 4 hours.

Nutrition:

Calories: 255

Carbs: 52g

Fat: 5g

Protein: 10g

# CHAPTER 8:

# Soups & Stews

## 37.  Southwest Corn Chowder

Preparation time: 15 minutes

Cooking time: 6 hours

Servings: 4

Ingredients:

- ¼ cup butter

- 1 onion, diced

- 1 jalapeno, minced

- 1 cup diced tomato

- 2 medium russet potatoes, peeled and diced

- 2 (15-ounce) cans creamed corn

- 2 cups of water

- 2 cups of milk

- 1 tsp. chili powder

- 1 tsp. cumin

- ¼ tsp. cayenne pepper

- Salt and pepper, to taste

Directions:

1. Melt the butter on Sauté. Add the onion, jalapeno, and cook for 3 minutes. Add rest of the ingredients and cover. Cook on low for 6 hours. Serve.

Nutrition: Calories 437 Carbs 69g at 16g Protein 12g

# 38.  Mediterranean Vegetable Stew

Preparation time: 15 minutes

Cooking time: 6 hours

Servings: 6

Ingredients:

- 2 tbsps. olive oil

- 4 garlic cloves, chopped

- 1 red onion, chopped

- 1 red bell pepper, seeded and chopped

- 1 eggplant, chopped

- 1 (15-ounce) can artichokes, drained and chopped

- 1/3 cup kalamata olives, pitted and chopped

- 2 (15-ounce) cans diced tomatoes

- 4 cups vegetable broth

- 1 tsp. red pepper flakes

- ½ tsp. dried oregano

- ½ tsp. dried parsley

- 1 tsp. salt

- ½ tsp. pepper

Directions:

1. Add everything in the crock pot. Cover and cook on low for 6 hours. Serve.

Nutrition:

Calories 214

Carbs 31g

Fat 6g

Protein 6g

# 39.  White Bean and Tomato Stew

Preparation time: 15 minutes

Cooking time: 6 hours & 30 minutes

Servings: 4

Ingredients:

- 1 (15-ounce) can cannellini beans, drained

- 4 cups vegetable broth

- 1 tbsp. butter

- 1 tsp. salt

- 2 cloves garlic, minced

- ½ tsp. dried sage

- ¼ tsp. dried thyme

- ½ tsp. black pepper

- 1 cup tomato, diced

Directions:

1. Add everything in the crock pot except for tomato. Cover and cook on low for 6 hours. Open and add tomato, stir and cook for 30 minutes more. Serve.

Nutrition:

Calories 128

Carbs 20g

Fat 4g

Protein 6g

# 40.   Curried Seitan Stew

Preparation time: 15 minutes

Cooking time: 4 hours

Servings: 4

Ingredients:

- 2 tbsps. butter

- ½ onion, chopped

- 2 cloves garlic, minced

- 1 tsp. fresh ginger, minced

- 2 tbsp. Panang curry paste

- 1 tsp. paprika

- 1 tsp. sugar

- ½ tsp. cayenne pepper

- 1 tsp. soy sauce
- 14-ounces of milk
- 3 cups vegetable broth
- 2 cups seitan, cubed
- ½ tsp. salt
- ¼ tsp. pepper
- ¼ cup cilantro, chopped

Directions:

1. Add everything in the crock pot except for the cilantro. Cover and cook on low for 4 hours. Garnish with cilantro and serve.

Nutrition:Calories 322 Carbs 16g Fat 28g Protein 6.5g

# 41.   Seitan and Cabbage Stew

Preparation time: 15 minutes

Cooking time: 6 hours

Servings: 4

Ingredients:

- 1 onion, chopped

- 1 carrot, chopped

- 2 celery ribs, chopped

- 4 cups cabbage, shredded

- 2 potatoes, chopped

- 3 cups seitan, cubed

- 4 cups vegetable broth

- 2 tbsps. Worcestershire sauce

- ½ tsp. salt

- ¼ tsp. black pepper

Directions:

1. Add everything in the crock pot and cover. Cook on low for 6 hours. Open and serve.

Nutrition:

Calories 232

Carbs 28g

Fat 1g

Protein 13g

# CHAPTER 9:

# Snacks

## 42.   Creamy Mustard Asparagus

Preparation Time: 10 minutes

Cooking Time: 3 hours

Servings: 2

Ingredients:

- 1 lb. asparagus, trimmed and halved

- 2 teaspoons of mustard

- ¼ cup of coconut cream

- 2 garlic cloves, minced

- 1 tablespoon of chives, diced

- Salt and black pepper- to taste

Directions:

1. Start by throwing all the ingredients into the Crockpot. Cover its lid and cook for 3 hours on Low setting.

2. Once done, remove its lid of the crockpot carefully. Mix well and garnish as desired. Serve warm.

Nutrition:

Calories 149

Fat 14.5 g

Carbs 10.6 g

Protein 2.6 g

## 43.   Savory Pine Nuts Cabbage

Preparation Time: 10 minutes   Cooking Time: 2 hours

Servings: 2

Ingredients:

- 1 savoy cabbage, shredded

- 2 tablespoons of avocado oil

- 1 tablespoon of balsamic vinegar

- ¼ cup of pine nuts, toasted

- ½ cup of vegetable broth

- Salt and black pepper- to taste

Directions:

1. Start by throwing all the ingredients into the Crockpot. Cover its lid and cook for 2 hours on Low setting.

2. Once done, remove its lid of the crockpot carefully. Mix well and garnish as desired. Serve warm.

Nutrition:

Calories 145

Fat 13.1 g

Carbs 4 g

Protein 3.5 g

# 44.   Nutmeg Fennel

Preparation Time: 10 minutes

Cooking Time: 3 hours

Servings: 2

Ingredients:

- 2 fennel bulbs, sliced

- 2 tablespoon of olive oil

- 4 garlic cloves, diced

- 2 tablespoons of balsamic vinegar

- 2 and ½ cups of baby spinach

- ½ teaspoon of nutmeg, ground

- ¼ cup of vegetable broth

Directions:

1. Start by throwing all the ingredients into the Crockpot. Cover its lid and cook for 3 hours on Low setting.

2. Once done, remove its lid of the crockpot carefully. Mix well and garnish as desired. Serve warm.

Nutrition:

Calories 244

Fat 24.8 g

Carbs 2.1 g

Protein 24 g

# 45.  Herbed Cherry Tomatoes

Preparation Time: 10 minutes

Cooking Time: 1 hour

Servings: 2

Ingredients:

- 4 garlic cloves, minced

- A pinch of salt and black pepper

- 2 lbs. Cherry tomatoes halved

- 2 tablespoon of olive oil

- 1 tablespoon of dill, diced

- ½ cups of chicken stock

- ¼ cup of basil, diced

Directions:

1. Start by throwing all the ingredients into the Crockpot. Cover its lid and cook for 1 hour on Low setting.

2. Once done, remove its lid of the crockpot carefully. Mix well and garnish as desired. Serve warm.

Nutrition:

Calories 145

Fat 13.1 g

Carbs 4 g

Protein 3.5 g

# 46.   Viennese Coffee

Preparation Time: 10 minutes   Cooking Time: 2.5 hours

Servings: 2

Ingredients:

- 3 cups of strong brewed coffee

- 3 tablespoons of sugar-free chocolate syrup

- 1 teaspoon of stevia

- 1/3 cup of heavy whipping cream

- 1/4 cup of crème de cacao

- Whipped cream, optional

Directions:

1. Start by throwing all the ingredients into the Crockpot. Cover its lid and cook for 2.5 hours on Low setting.

2. Once done, remove its lid of the crockpot carefully. Garnish with whipped cream. Serve warm.

Nutrition:

Calories 231

Fat 32.9 g

Carbs 9.1 g

Protein 4.4 g

# CHAPTER 10:

# Desserts

## 47.  Chocolate Cake

Preparation time: 15 minutes

Cooking time: 6 hours

Servings: 4

Ingredients:

- 1 box instant Chocolate Pudding Mix

- 4 eggs

- 1 box Chocolate or Devil's Food Cake Mix

- 8 ounces sour Cream

- ¾ cup vegetable oil

- 1 cup water

- Cooking spray

Directions:

1. Coat the crock pot with cooking spray. Mix all the remaining ingredients together, and pour into crock pot. Cook on high for 3 hours or on low for 6 hours.

Nutrition:

Calories 605

Fat 43 g

Carbs 46 g

Protein 8 g

# 48.   Monkey Bread

Preparation time: 15 minutes

Cooking time: 2 hours

Servings: 6

Ingredients:

- 1 teaspoon cinnamon

- 1 cup brown sugar

- ¼ cup butter, melted

- 1 tube biscuits like Pillsbury Biscuits

Directions:

1. Break biscuits into the pre-cut pieces. Mix the brown sugar and cinnamon. Dip biscuit pieces into melted butter. Put buttered biscuit into a bowl of cinnamon and brown sugar until fully coat.

2.  Place the pieces into crock pot until you have all of the pieces layered in the crock pot. Pour extra brown sugar and cinnamon on top. Cook on low for 2 hours. Serve.

Nutrition:

Calories 368

Fat 9.2 g

Carbs 68.1 g

Protein 5.1 g

# 49.  Cranberry Walnut Stuffed Apples

Preparation time: 15 minutes

Cooking time: 4-5 hours

Servings: 4-6

Ingredients:

- ¾ cup walnuts, toasted and chopped

- ½ cup dried cranberries, chopped

- 1/3 cup packed light brown sugar

- 1/3 cup rolled oats 3 tablespoons unsalted butter, diced

- 1 tablespoon fresh lemon juice

- ½ teaspoon ground cinnamon

- Kosher salt

- 4 large or 6 medium firm baking apples (such as Rome, Golden Delicious or Honey Crisp)

- 1 cup apple cider

- Vanilla ice cream and pure maple syrup, for serving

Directions:

1. In a small mixing bowl, combine the walnuts, cranberries, brown sugar, oats, butter, lemon juice, cinnamon, and salt.

2. Using your clean hands, mush the ingredients together until well combined. Core the apples, being sure to leave the bottoms and sides intact.

3. Stuff the apples with the nut mixture and place them in the crock pot. Pour apple cider over all the apples.

4. Cook on low for 4–5 hours or until the apples are soft. The time may vary depending on the size of your

apples. Serve with a scoop of ice cream and or maple syrup if desired.

Nutrition: Calories 177 at 5.6 g Carbs 33.6 g rotein 2.8 g

# 50. Caramel Flan

Preparation time: 15 minutes

Cooking time: 4 hours

Servings: 4

Ingredients:

- 3 large eggs

- 1½ cups whole milk

- ½ tablespoon vanilla extract

- 1¼ cups granulated sugar, divided

- 8 ounce can sweeten condensed milk

- Hot water

Directions:

1. Warm a small saucepan on the stove over medium heat. Pour in 1 cup sugar. Stir until sugar melts.

Remove from the heat, and spoon evenly the liquid caramel into each of 4 ramekins. Set aside.

2. Whisk eggs in a large bowl. Add condensed and whole milk, and the remaining ¼ cup sugar. Strain the mixture through cheesecloth. Pour over caramel in the ramekins.

3. Set the ramekins in the crock pot. Carefully pour in hot water to surround them. Cover and cook for 4 hours on high. Carefully lift out the flans, and let them cool on a wire rack for an hour.

4. Serve. Run a knife around the edge of each ramekin and flip the chilled flans upside down into serving plates.

Nutrition:Calories 223 Fat 6 g

Carbs 35 g Protein 7 g

# Conclusion

You have to the end of this amazing cookbook, but always remember that this is not the end of your cooking journey with the crockpot; but instead, this is your stepping stone towards more cooking glory. We hope you have found your favorite recipes that are time-saving and money-saving.

Now that you know how Crockpot works and the many benefits of using it, maybe it is time for you to buy one for your family, in case you haven't owned one. When it comes to time spent preparing meals for your family, Crock-Pot is a lifesaver. If you are a busy person, a powerful solution is to use the crockpot.

You will also love to own one if you want to make your life simpler at work if you want to make your life simpler at home, and if you want to preserve some of the natural resources. You could also use one if you want to lean towards a healthier lifestyle as cooking in the crockpot is conducive to health than in the oven.

The crockpot can be used in making homemade and custom-made buffets, even in catering services. You can use it for cooking for your staff for special occasions and for showing them how to cook a tasty and healthier dish for your guests well within their own crockpot.

After choosing the best one for you, maybe it is time for you to know more about the recipes you should use. There are various recipes in this cookbook that are perfect for crockpot cooking, and they will definitely be useful and beneficial for you.

Moreover, whether you are a newbie or an experienced cook, you are going to love this cookbook as it is packed with every conceivable taste. You have discovered more than 1000 recipes in this cookbook that you can put into practice using your crockpot. You can always customize the recipes to suit your taste buds, as you can make any recipe mild or hot, sweet or sour; you have all the freedom to make the recipes your own. The best thing about cooking using a crockpot is that you just need to add the main ingredients, and no other complicated cooking preparation is needed; the crockpot will add most of the other ingredients for you.

This crockpot cookbook covered all the recipes that are sure to make your heart happy and your taste buds happy as well. These meals are not just easy to make, but they will also save you hours of preparation and cleanup. The crockpot is also famous for its great nutritional value. It is the best nutritional value you will ever get. The high levels of healthy fats, proteins, and fiber you get when you cook using the crockpot are entirely natural, which everybody needs. Some of the ingredients are healthy enough to be consumed on their own.